Lessons in Leadership

Sharing the Wisdom of

Great Hotel General Managers

Marylouise Fitzgibbon Ph.D.

Contents

INTRODUCTION

In my first book, *450 Things Every Hotel General Manager Should Know*, I compiled a master list of all the operational tactics I had learned in my 25 years in the hotel business. I spent the first 10 years working my way up in hotels, including 8 different management jobs in a variety of operations and support roles. During that time, I kept a running list of all the great questions I heard various leaders ask and all the things I wanted to make sure I remembered when I became a General Manager. For the next 15 years in my career, I worked as a General Manager at 5 different hotels, ranging from midscale to luxury, and then as a Regional General Manager, overseeing a portfolio of 10,000+ hotel rooms and 5,000+ employees. Throughout that time, I continued to refine the list. That book could have been titled *1000+ Things Every Hotel General Manager Should Know*! Instead, I narrowed the list down to those things that I believe will be most critical to your success as a Hotel General Manager.

The response to that book was incredible, and I was humbled by all the messages I received from readers, that it really helped them with the OPERATIONAL TACTICS they needed, in order to be successful in this business. But along with that focus on operations, it is equally as important, to focus on LEADERSHIP CONCEPTS. I was fortunate over the course of my hotel career to *work for,* then to *work alongside,* and eventually to *supervise over* many incredible General Managers. From each of these leaders, I wrote down the unique ways in which they focused on LEADERSHIP within their hotels. While each had their own approach, I found that there were common themes in how all these great leaders 'led' their hotels. Those 18 themes then became the basis for this book. As I was writing this book, it occurred to me that these leadership themes were applicable to any organization, *not just hotels*. With that in mind, you'll note that I keep the guidance generic, and not specific to just running hotels. My hope is that will then allow you to apply the knowledge to any business you choose to lead, not just within the hotel industry.

Throughout this book, I refer to the word LEADER, not to indicate a position of power, or a title on a business card. Instead, when I use the word leader, I am referring to the leader inside all of us. The leader in YOU. People follow great leaders because they respect them, not because they have power. Leadership doesn't come because of a title, it is earned. John Maxwell said, "If you think you are leading, but no one is following, then you are only taking a walk."

For this book, I created a simple 3-step model; *Leading Yourself, Leading Others, and Leading an Organization*. This is based on the premise that you cannot improve anything at an organizational level until you have credibility at an individual level, then a team level. Great leadership can be learned. Everything starts with just one step, one new learning. This book is broken down into small, key learnings. A mantra that has helped me throughout my own leadership journey is: *Just Do the Next Thing*. Implement just one of the practices in this guide, and then the next, and the next, and so forth. Slow and steady wins the race, one concept at a time. Best of luck to you!

-Marylouise Fitzgibbon, Ph.D.

LEADING YOURSELF

1. SELF-AWARENESS

Any discussion on leadership must start with the basic premise that in order to lead *others*, you must first dig deep to understand who *you are* as a person. Not the person that you want the world to see, but who you really are and what you value. At the core. The more you focus on getting to this basic understanding of yourself, the more you are able to take your gifts, your strengths, your talents, and fully use them to improve the lives of those around you.
☐

The process of gaining a deeper understanding of yourself, begins with self-awareness. Often referred to as emotional intelligence, this process is about a core understanding of how you are perceived by others. Individuals with high levels of emotional intelligence are able to recognize their own emotions and those of others, and then use that information to guide thinking and behavior. They can discern between different feelings and use that information to self-regulate and make adjustments to adapt to various situations.

This type of self-awareness then leads to being seen as more authentic by others. Authentic people accept themselves and others for the way they are, while still focusing on ways to improve. They use humor to improve a situation, not to harm anyone. They are able to express their emotions clearly, not in an emotional way. They quickly admit to making mistakes, and then learn from them. They don't look to others for approval or to feel valued. Authentic people don't use humor as a passive-aggressive approach to pointing out the weaknesses of others. They learn from mistakes and they don't get defensive if someone shares feedback on ways in which they might improve a certain aspect of themselves.

Authentic leaders know when to be vulnerable and when to be firm, understanding that both are necessary for effective leadership. They also recognize that authenticity requires courage—courage to stand by your values, make difficult decisions, and sometimes face criticism for being true to yourself. Ultimately, authentic leadership fosters a culture of openness, respect, and mutual trust, creating an environment where both leaders and their teams can thrive.

The goal is to continually learn more about who you are at the core, and then match that to what people consistently see on a regular basis. As you close the gap on those two worlds, you begin to show the world your authentic, unique self. This is where you find your own voice. One that is honest and sincere. This is where you stop sounding like someone you're not. Where you let who you are, where you come from, and what you value, shine through when you speak. People want, respect, and will follow authentic leadership. Forget about being perfect or being the kind of person you think others expect you to be. Instead, focus on being 'real', and don't disguise who you are. People will never willingly follow someone they feel is inauthentic.

2. RELATIONSHIPS

Behind every business, there are people, and people function in society via relationships. Leadership is a series of relationships. Sometimes the relationship is one-to-many, and sometimes it's one-to-one. But regardless of whether the number is 1 or 1,000, leadership *is* based on relationships. The connections with your employees, partners, customers, and vendors are all a series of relationships that need to be built based on trust and communication. Building relationships should not be confused with the simple act of socializing or giving everyone you know your business card. Instead, it is about engaging and getting to know others. Time and effort are required. Putting the time in to get to know those that you work with is essential to a productive work environment.

True relationship-building goes beyond superficial interactions and delves into understanding and valuing the individual contributions of each person involved. It involves active listening, empathy, and genuine interest in the well-being and aspirations of others. This kind of investment in relationships fosters a sense of belonging and loyalty. When people feel understood and appreciated, they are more likely to go the extra mile, collaborate effectively, and support each other in achieving common goals. People first want to know that you value them, before they are able to truly contribute to the work. Taking the time to create this type of culture will pay off greatly, as the strength of these relationships often determines the resilience of a team in the face of challenges.

Relationships are the building blocks for attaining results, both for yourself and for others. Informal relationships should be based on honesty and respect, and not for personal gain. Relationships certainly cannot solve every problem, but they can lead to increased trust, which then creates an environment in which issues can be solved. As you authentically engage with others, you are able to form partnerships and foster collaboration that are vital to success. Success in your life or in business often boils down to how well you interact with others. Relationships are what open the door. With poor relationships come burned bridges, and with burned bridges, you simply can't be effective no matter how 'right you are'. Therefore, cultivating and maintaining healthy relationships is crucial for both your long-term professional success as well as your own personal fulfillment. The strength of your relationships ultimately will determine the strength of your overall impact.

The cultivation of meaningful relationships is a continuous process that requires consistent effort and attention. It involves recognizing and addressing conflicts in a constructive manner, celebrating successes together, and providing support during difficult times. Building and maintaining these relationships also requires you to have a humble approach, as well as a willingness to learn and grow from your interactions with others. Great leaders find that when they prioritize relationships and take the time to nurture them, they are able to create a powerful network of trust and cooperation. Those relationships help to drive not just your own success but success for the organization.

3. OPTIMISM

People want to follow someone that provides hope for the future and brings joy to the situation. Winston Churchill said, "A pessimist sees the difficulty in every opportunity; an optimist sees the opportunity in every difficulty." Optimism should not be confused with unrealistic and wishful thinking. Instead, it's about beginning with a dose of realism, and building a brighter future from there. It is an attitude that a leader projects, conveying the belief that the outcomes the team is working towards will be favorable. Leaders who focus on optimism find ways to align their teams behind a common goal. A goal they see as not just a stretch, but rather as highly likely.

Optimism in leadership acts as a catalyst for motivation and perseverance. When leaders approach challenges with a positive outlook, it sets a tone for the entire team. This attitude helps to create a culture where employees feel more confident in their abilities and are more willing to take on challenges without the fear of failure. Optimistic leaders inspire their teams to envision success and work collectively towards it, fostering a sense of unity and shared purpose. This collective belief in a positive outcome not only boosts morale but also enhances overall performance, as team members are more inclined to invest their best efforts when they believe in the potential for success.

Martin Seligman, Ph.D., known as the founder of Positive Psychology, defines optimism as 'the proactive response to challenges, characterized by a strong sense of confidence and personal competence'. His research has found that optimistic individuals are able to confront challenges, with an underlying belief that they will overcome them. This then leads to an empowered outlook on life. Positive Psychology focuses on the strengths of any situation. With this outlook, the positive outcomes are highlighted, and with it, an acknowledgement of the efforts that led to those results. When you lead with optimism, it shows your entire team the importance of having the right mindset when navigating challenges. This approach not only enhances individual performance but also fosters a collaborative and supportive team environment. Optimism can be contagious, spreading through the team and creating a culture where obstacles are seen as opportunities for growth rather than insurmountable barriers. By championing an optimistic perspective, leaders can inspire resilience, drive innovation, and cultivate a work atmosphere that thrives on positive reinforcement and collective progress.

Optimistic people believe that adverse events are temporary, limited in scope (as opposed to present in every aspect of a person's life), and manageable. Research shows that optimistic people tend to be far more resilient in the face of adversity. They treat failure as a natural part of life and as an opportunity for improvement. That process then helps them to learn and keep moving closer to achieving their goals. People are naturally drawn to leaders that are upbeat and have a positive attitude. Even if optimism isn't something you naturally lean towards, it is something that can be developed. Life stress can be tough, but leaders can offset that and build positive momentum by creating a positive environment for those they interact with.

4. COMMUNICATION

Colin Powell once said, "great leaders are almost always great simplifiers, who can cut through argument, debate and doubt, to offer a solution everybody can understand". Great communication begins with identifying which messages are important, and then finding creative ways to get that information to the people that need to know. Direct communication is often the most critical. The more you can remove *the telephone game* and communicate directly with the individuals who need the information, the better. Consider how quickly you can provide information to your team, so that everyone feels in the know. This becomes even more important when communicating in a virtual setting.

The most important information you can share with your team is your vision, your priorities, and your plan to get there. Those key messages need to be repeated over and over. When a leader is able to communicate their vision and priorities clearly (without clutter and buzzwords), it allows the team to fully understand what needs to be done to achieve the goals. If your team doesn't know where you are going and where you are trying to take them, they will have a hard time getting excited about the journey. It is especially important to have a compelling vision that provides direction and focuses everyone's energy on getting where they are headed.

A cornerstone of effective communication is fostering an environment of active listening and feedback. Communication is not just about the leader sending messages to the team, but also about understanding the perspectives and concerns of the employees. Great leaders encourage open dialogue and create forums to solicit ongoing feedback from everyone. Communication is a two-way-street. Listen to your employees so they feel that they are truly part of the success of the business. Employees can offer invaluable insights on how things can run better. Leaders who actively listen to their employees create an environment of respect. This in turn promotes a sense of ownership and collective decision-making. When leaders acknowledge and addressing concerns promptly, you build trust and strengthen relationships within the team.

A great way to enhance communication is to leverage technology. Particularly important the larger an organization gets, a leader must consistently look for new tools to disseminate information to all levels. The same tools can often be used in reverse, to gather feedback from the front lines and get it back to the top. Keep in mind that technology can never replace old fashioned human connections. Leaders who are visible within their operation, walking around, building rapport, listening, asking questions, and creating a sense of belonging, will always have the strongest communication channels, with real-time information.

Jack Welch was legendary for demanding fast, simple communication of his entire team, and once said "insecure managers create complexity". Not only should you consider how to convey information clearly, but you should think about how to tailor the message to various audiences, to ensure it's hitting the mark. Don't overcomplicate communication; figure out what information matters, and get it to the people that need to know.

5. ORGANIZATION

Life is made up of a series of priorities, which make it imperative that you are able to stay organized within your personal life, and at work. One visual that has consistently helped me is based on an old story of a professor who placed a glass jar on his desk and proceeded to fill it with rocks and sand in front of the students. I think of my personal and work priorities as the big rocks, and everything else as the sand. If I fill my life (my glass jar) with the non-essential work (sand), then there is no room for the big rocks (my priorities). So instead, I keep an ongoing list of what my big rocks are at both work and in my personal life. I look at that list every single day, so that 'sand' can't take over my day. This method allows me to stay organized on what matters, and greatly reduces stress, while increasing my productivity, both at work, and at home. I often share this glass jar story with my teams as a way to encourage them to focus on the priorities in their life, versus letting the crisis-of-the moment take over.

Another significant advantage of being organized is the heightened sense of control it gives you. When tasks, deadlines, and priorities are clearly defined and managed, your team will feel empowered to do what needs to be done to achieve those goals. By fostering a culture of organization and efficiency, you can unlock the full potential of your team, driving innovation, collaboration, and sustained success. Simply put, being organized as a leader, means that the things that matter the most to your organization and to your employees are what gets focused on.

An organized leader sets a standard for efficiency and attention to detail, which in turn reduces the likelihood of mistakes and oversights. When everything is in order, processes run smoothly, deadlines are met, and resources are utilized effectively. This creates a stable work environment where your employees can focus on their tasks without the distractions caused by disorganization. An organized leader can also serve as a role model, showing the entire team the importance of being having things in order, leading to a clear focus on the priorities. This type of environment helps to ensure that everyone is aligned and working towards common goals.

We don't realize how much time can be wasted when things are chaotic and disorganized. This small shift in mindset can literally transform your life. Find a way to better organize your emails, your texts, your calendar. Spend the energy on figuring this out, as it will save you an incredible amount of time in the long run. Don't leave this to chance, find a system that works for you. Use a variety of tools, techniques, and methods to find an organizational system that you can sustain.

On a personal note, one of the things that causes most people to be unorganized is the feeling that there is just too much to focus on. A technique that has helped me immensely is this: make a list of everything on your mind.. Now take that list and divide it into three topics. *Things I have total control over. Things I have some control over. Things I have no control over.* Get organized around making a plan for the 'total control' list, and 'some control' list. And then force yourself to move the 'no control' items out of your mind. They are likely taking up valuable brain space that should be focused on the other areas of your life.

6. WELLNESS

Most experts on wellness suggest that individuals should focus on 5 aspects of health; *physical, mental, emotional, social, and spiritual.* Physical health includes regular exercise, a balanced diet, and adequate sleep. Mental health includes effective stress management. Emotional health focuses on understanding and managing one's emotions, as well as self-awareness and resilience. Social health involves maintaining strong personal connections and positive interactions with others. Spiritual health typically focuses on finding meaning and purpose in life as well as inner peace.

Working full time while caring for our loved ones can often mean that we put our own self-care and wellness last on the priority list. Health and work don't have to be mutually exclusive. In order to operate at my best, I know that I must optimize my own self-care. For me, there are six personal priorities that keep me balanced: *prayer, exercise, healthy eating, proper sleep, quality family time, and working on a personal goal.* What are yours? Take a moment to write them down right now. Steven Covey once said "Be patient with yourself. Self-growth is holy ground, there is no greater investment". Identify what your personal priorities are, so that your self-care is just as high on your 'to-do' list as everything else.

A key component of Wellness is focusing on work-life-integration. Even in industries that are known for long hours, and a breakneck pace, some level of balance can be achieved. Old school leadership suggested that we should check our family lives at the door when we arrive at the office, that work and family were two separate ledgers in zero-sum competition with each other. But we know from experience that's not the way the world works. Kids get sick at school, aging parents need additional care, and clients/bosses have urgent questions that can't wait until Monday. But it *is* possible to deliver great work while integrating our personal lives in. We need to resist a culture that even implies otherwise.

Wellness also means showing up each day as your Best Self. Once you accept that only you have the power to change yourself, it unlocks a world of possibilities for you. Take the time to pause and reflect on the areas of your life that you'd like to improve. Where are you spending your time? Are the foods you are eating contributing to your health? What people are you spending your time with? Once you are truly honest with where you are at, and where you want to be, cut the negative self-talk out of your life. A mantra that has helped me in my personal journey of Wellness is *Just Do The Next Thing.* Steps towards Wellness can often be daunting, but breaking things down to just the *next* positive thing can make things much more manageable.

Focusing on your Best Self requires a realization that you have been given a specific set of skills and talents that are unique to you. Don't compare yourself to others. While it's important to recognize your areas of improvement, it's even more important to focus on building on your strengths. You are fully capable of teaching your brain to think positively about yourself, and the future choices that you will make. As you focus on becoming your Best Self, you slowly become the person you were meant to be!

LEADING OTHERS

7. SERVANT LEADERSHIP

As many organizations have shifted their focus from profit at all costs to social responsibility, a growing interest has occurred in exploring the topic of Servant Leadership. Servant Leaders view ethical behavior as a critically important factor and work to create an ethical environment within their organizations. This type of leader puts the needs of others first, through a strong desire to serve others. Servant Leaders focus on the well-being and development of their teams. This approach contrasts with traditional leadership models that emphasize hierarchical power and control.

While those older leadership models tend to view the leader at the top of the pyramid, Servant Leadership focuses on a hierarchy with an upside-down pyramid. The leader's primary goal is to help people develop themselves to reach their potential. By placing the employees at the top of the theoretical pyramid, they become the primary focus. For businesses that are heavily focused on customer service, Servant Leadership is the link that translates how an employee is treated (served) with how the employee then treats (serves) the customer. When the desire to serve others permeates an organization, the benefits can reach everyone that the organization serves, especially customers.

Servant Leaders focus on personal attributes such as humility, compassion, integrity, vision, mentorship, and patience. Those are definitely not the same characteristics as a command-and-control leadership, but Servant Leaders lead their teams with a clear sense of purpose and ethical standards. Servant Leaders focus on putting others first, and serving them rather than seeking to be served. It's all about prioritizing the needs and well-being of those you lead. That translates into focusing on the growth and development of others, and helping them to realize their potential and achieve their goals.

Many authors have concluded that Jesus Christ is the definitive example of Servant Leadership. Regardless of one's religious affiliations, it is well documented that Jesus was an excellent leader. He gathered a group of 12 men who were unqualified for the work that he was asking them to do and rallied them around a vision and purpose that continues today. Jesus often spoke to his disciples about serving others. The most powerful of his Servant Leader teachings are found in the Gospel of Mark. In these teachings, Jesus states: "If anyone wants to be first, he shall be last of all and servant of all". In the following chapter, He continues teaching with: "But it shall not be so among you. Rather, whoever wishes to be great among you will be your servant". The concept of *Leading like Jesus* is something that resonates deeply with me, and has served as a true north for me, in my own leadership journey.

8. DIVERSITY, INCLUSION, & BELONGING

Any discussion on leading others must include an understanding of the role that we play in fostering diversity, inclusion, and belonging. Leaders need to be the champion for ensuring that it is embedded in the culture of the team. Verna Meyers once said, "Diversity is being invited to the party, but inclusion is being asked to dance." Another author then added, "and belonging is feeling free to dance however you want". A great way to do this is to broaden your own cultural and social horizons beyond your usual experiences. Learning to see life from different perspectives will give you greater flexibility in problem solving. Creating an environment where diverse voices are represented, and everyone feels included and has a sense of belonging is a critical leadership skill.

Research has shown that team members who feel like their diverse perspectives are valued and that they truly belong, results in a substantial increase in job performance. Incorporating diverse viewpoints also results in better decision-making. If a diverse group of employees is hired and then invited to the table to help make important decisions, but there hasn't been an investment in creating a sense of belonging, many of those employees may not feel comfortable expressing opposing ideas. Having a seat at the table is not enough. Leaders need to create an environment where everyone on the team feels comfortable speaking up without fear. By creating a culture of belonging, your team won't feel the need to downplay their identities.

It's important that you encourage your employees to participate actively. Employees need to feel included, which then leads to higher engagement and motivation. Yes, it's the right thing to do, but also, employees who feel like they belong tend to be significantly more satisfied with their jobs, which leads to higher retention rates. That in turn means they are less likely to leave for other opportunities, reducing your turnover costs. When individuals feel connected to their workplace, they are more committed to their roles and invested in the organization's success. Furthermore, active participation fosters a sense of ownership and accountability among employees, as they feel their contributions directly impact the company's outcomes. This sense of ownership can drive creativity and innovation, as team members are more likely to share their ideas and take initiative. Additionally, a culture of inclusivity and active participation can enhance teamwork and collaboration, as employees from diverse backgrounds and perspectives work together towards common goals. By promoting active participation, leaders can build a more dynamic, resilient, and forward-thinking organization.

Not only is a sense of belonging good for your team, it is also a driver for innovation within your organization. By encouraging your employees to share their unique ideas and perspectives, it can drive much higher levels of creative problem-solving within your team. When employees feel their diverse backgrounds and experiences are valued, they are more likely to bring their own innovated ideas to the table. In essence, fostering a sense of belonging not only strengthens team cohesion but also cultivates an innovative culture where diverse ideas can flourish.

9. DEVELOPING OTHERS

Developing others is a key skill that leaders must focus on. Don't assume that everyone knows the skills and traits that you are looking for, that will take them to the next level. Work with each person on your team to identify their strengths as well as areas of development. Then help them to make a plan to focus on those things. This activity is particularly important for the high performers on the team. Ensure they know that you see them as top talent, and that you are invested in their development. Determine who can grow and learn from taking on new assignments, and train them according to your expectations.

Once you have trained your team and you trust that they understand what needs to be done, allow them to do their work without your interference. Micromanaging how someone does a task demotivates them. However, the buy-in that is created when someone has the autonomy to ideate and create something on their own, simply cannot be achieved through you *telling* them how to do the job. Once expectations have been set, assign tasks and then get out of the way! Your leadership will not be defined by what you accomplish, but by how you developed your team, and what they were able to accomplish. Sharing your knowledge, and teaching others is a big part of any leader's job. Think about your experiences, draw lessons from what you know, and then figure out a variety of methods to share those lessons with your team; formally and informally.

A phrase that I often use when talking about development with my teams is *Teachable Moments*. These are small moments where I am able to share a lesson I have learned. Often these take the form of a story where I failed at something and then found a better path afterwards. Teachable Moments are the primary way that I develop my teams. They are typically done during a staff meeting or during a one-on-one meeting with one of my direct reports. If you're not using this format, I highly recommend it. It is based on humility, showing your team a more vulnerable side of you. It is also a simple way to take the learnings that you have gathered over the years, and passing them along.

If you're not sure where to start with developing your team, a method I often suggest is to simply write down categories of areas you believe each person could benefit from. Some categories may be universal across all members of your team (eg. communication, problem-solving, delegation). Other categories should be unique to the individual, and targeted towards the items that you believe they could benefit from development on. Once you've created those categories, make a second column to identify the best way to provide that development to each person. Sometimes a training class is the best method. Other times, they would benefit most from simply hearing your thoughts on that topic, as well as how you've personally developed in that area over the years. And don't forget the power of simple Teachable Moments! Carving 10 minutes out of every staff meeting or one-on-one to discuss that particular area of development with your team, is an incredibly effective way to create a culture of continuous development with your team.

10. GIVING FEEDBACK

Bill Gates said "We all need people who will give us feedback. That's how we improve." Most people naturally want to succeed in their work and providing them with feedback helps them to understand how their performance compares to the expectations of their role. Most individuals aren't looking for a pat on the back accompanied by a "good job." Rather, they want to hear the truth about how they can improve. In many studies, people actually prefer corrective feedback to purely praise and recognition. Your employees want to constantly improve, and feedback helps them get there. Feedback gives people an opportunity to look at themselves in a different light. It helps them see how others perceive them, and how that perception might be positively or negatively impacting them.

Too often, feedback is something that happens only once a year, during annual reviews or appraisals. A feedback-rich culture, where people are comfortable asking for and receiving feedback from their colleagues and managers, can really change how a workplace operates. Though receiving feedback can be daunting for people, it's also absolutely necessary if you want to create motivated and high-performing teams. When giving people constructive feedback, it's best to break it into four sections; *describe the situation, describe the behavior, explain the outcome of the behavior, and discuss alternate actions for next time.* Anytime you have to give constructive feedback to someone, always describe the facts of the situation without judgement. Only focus on the behavior that you want corrected, not the attitude. It's far more immediate and effective to adjust observable employee behavior than it is to attempt to adjust attitudes. Tell people in clear terms what the feedback is that needs to be addressed, don't talk in roundabout circles- just be honest. Never point out the weaknesses of someone in front of others. Praise publicly but provide constructive feedback privately.

Although the topic of 'giving feedback' tends to focus on areas of improvement, I've personally found it far more effective to focus on the areas where each member of my team is doing well. Each individual has been given a unique set of strengths and talents. And often those strengths are different than mine. If I focus my energy on pointing out how individuals on my team are doing things differently than I would have done it, I am missing the point. Instead, my role is to highlight their strengths, and find ways for them to showcase those strengths more often.

An earlier chapter discussed Positive Psychology, and 'giving feedback' is another area where this concept can help you immensely, and not just at work. Positive Psychology has helped at work and also in my personal life. I spend far more time giving positive feedback to my spouse and my children, then I ever do in pointing out areas where they could improve. If this isn't something you naturally lean towards, I strongly encourage you to give it a try. The impact that you will almost immediately see in the quality of your relationships, can't be denied. People thrive in an environment where those around them focus on their strengths, not just their areas of opportunity. As a leader at work, at home, or in your friend-group, you have the unique opportunity to use positive feedback to watch those around you thrive!

11.   LISTENING & ASKING QUESTIONS

Listening is one of the core habits of leaders who connect well with their teams. Active listening ensures that information is accurately received and understood, reducing the chances of miscommunication and errors. Your highest priority as a leader can't be expressing *your* ideas and convincing others to buy into them. Whether it's one-on-ones or group meetings, listening well begins with being intentional. Effective listening starts with being fully present. This means focusing entirely on the other person, without distractions, like checking your phone or thinking about other tasks. Avoiding interruptions is crucial; allow the person to finish their thoughts before you respond. If what someone says sparks an idea in you, write it down, and discuss once they are finished.

The role of a leader is not to just simply listen, but to ask great questions. Questions help to clarify any points that may be unclear and shows that you are actively trying to understand the speaker's message. In particular, strategic questions allow for deeper context, and to further conversation. Asking open-ended questions can often lead to the best possible insights. Focus on things like: *What do I need to know?, Why do we have this problem?, How do we solve this problem?, What do you think?, Can you challenge my thinking here?* A great way to show that you've truly heard them is to say some version of "here's what I think you want me to know about this, did I get that right?"

Be genuinely interested in other people and encourage them to talk about themselves and how they are thinking about the topic at hand. Trying to understand the speaker's feelings and perspectives can deepen the connection and foster a more meaningful conversation. As you listen to your team, they should feel that their perspective is valued. Wherever possible, implement the ideas they share with you, as it helps to create a culture where everyone feels their insights are valued. Colin Powell once said "the day soldiers stop bringing you their problems is the day you have stopped leading them. They have either lost confidence that you can help them or concluded that you do not care. Either case is a failure of leadership".

Leaders need to listen not just to understand the topic at hand, but to connect the dots with other work. In various group meetings, as well as one-on-one meetings, the leader should listen for the interdependencies of each team's work. They can then encourage cross-functional collaboration between different teams. By listening to how various projects intersect, you can identify synergies, potential conflicts, and even overlaps in work. This helps in aligning efforts and ensuring that all teams are working towards the same organizational goals. Additionally, this approach fosters a culture of transparency and open communication, which can lead to increased trust and morale among team members. Ultimately, when you are able to connect the dots, it leads to more strategic thinking, innovative solutions and can drive the overall performance of your team.

12.   MOTIVATION & INSPIRATION

Great leaders are constantly looking for ways to motivate and inspire their teams. The easiest and often most effective way to do this is to create an environment that aims at positive communication. This is an environment that is focused on getting to know your team members on a personal level and recognizing the unique contributions that each brings. Your team will be motivated by understanding how the work that they are doing ties into the greater good as an important part of the company's overall goals and direction. An act as simple as thanking each individual for the work they are doing can have a tremendous impact on employee morale. Simplicity often trumps grand gestures. John Maxwell once said, "Leaders must be close enough to relate to others, but far enough ahead to motivate them." Recognize the contribution of others wherever possible.

Motivating a team is crucial for a leader because it directly influences the team's productivity, engagement, and overall job satisfaction. By creating an environment centered on positive communication, leaders can foster a culture where employees feel valued and understood. When leaders take the time to know their team members personally and acknowledge their unique contributions, it helps individuals see how their work aligns with the company's broader objectives. This understanding enhances their sense of purpose and belonging within the organization. Acts of recognition, even as simple as thanking someone for their effort, can significantly boost morale and motivation. This approach underscores the idea that simplicity often has a more profound impact than grand gestures. Effective leaders maintain a balance of relatability and forward-thinking to inspire and guide their teams. Recognizing and celebrating contributions not only motivates employees but also builds a cohesive, driven team that is committed to achieving collective goals.

While motivation can move your team closer to your desired cultural outcomes, inspiration, on the other hand, focuses on *why*. This is an important distinction because inspiration runs deep and compels people to take action, even when motivation wavers. It's not enough to share with your team what tasks need to be done; it's critical that they understand *why* you do what you do. When people know how their role fits into the greater *why*, they are more inspired to navigate obstacles and continually push forward toward hitting the goals you have set for the organization.

Leaders who focus on inspiring their teams allow their employees to unlock their individual potential. Research continues to show a strong connection between an employee's self-esteem and their job satisfaction. Therefore, it is essential to focus on motivating, inspiring, and building the self-esteem of everyone on the team. This involves recognizing their achievements, providing constructive feedback, and offering opportunities for growth and development. Your team needs to consistently hear that you believe in them and understand why success is possible. By fostering a culture of inspiration and belief, you can create a more resilient and driven team that is capable of achieving long-term success. This approach not only enhances individual performance but also strengthens the overall cohesion and morale of the team.

LEADING AN ORGANIZATION

13.   CREATING THE CULTURE

The culture of an organization is defined by how the employees feel about the organization, what it's like to work there, and how work gets done. The most effective visual I use with my teams is to draw a simple picture for them of an iceberg jetting out of the water. The part you can 'see' above the water is all the initiatives your organization is working on. The part of the iceberg that you can't 'see' under the water, is your culture. It's created over time, and it tends to be difficult to identify exactly what made the culture what it is. It's critical for leaders to understand that it is your responsibility to help shape and improve the culture of your organization. In fact, creating a positive culture is one of the most important things you can do. A positive culture not only boosts employee morale but also enhances productivity and job satisfaction, ultimately contributing to the organization's success.

While there are dozens of ways to foster a positive culture, the most effective methods I have experienced include clarity around the goals and mission, frequent and transparent communication, recognition of everyone's contributions, a spirit of fun, and the development of each individual to reach their unique potential. By implementing these strategies, leaders can build a supportive and dynamic work environment that encourages employees to thrive and perform at their best.

If you let culture go unmanaged, the best laid plans can go off the rails very quickly. A strong and positive organizational culture acts as the foundation upon which all other aspects of the business are built. Leaders should strive to create a culture of excellence, which is an environment where people love coming to work, but also paired with well-defined standards, accountability, and strong operational discipline. This combination not only fosters a positive work atmosphere but also ensures that employees are aligned with the company's objectives and expectations, driving consistent performance and continuous improvement. A culture focused on excellence cannot be vague. It is a purposeful plan to ensure that your vision, mission, and goals are communicated to your employees in a variety of ways that shows them how their roles and responsibilities align with the goals of your organization.

Culture is always the first place to start, as it will impact all other aspects of the business. A well-established culture enhances teamwork, boosts morale, and promotes a sense of belonging among employees. I have personally found that it can also be a critical differentiator in attracting and retaining top talent, as individuals are more likely to stay with a company where they feel valued and motivated. Spend a significant amount of time working on your culture as it will often determine the success of your organization, regardless of how effective your business strategy may be. Investing in culture means investing in the long-term health of the organization, ensuring that every team member is engaged, productive, and aligned with the overall vision and mission.

14.   BUSINESS ACUMEN

Leading an organization is all about delivering results, whatever those results may be. The most critical information for a leader to understand early on is what the key-performance-indicators (KPIs) are for the organization they are leading. These could be given from a corporate office, or your boss, or from the owner of your organization. KPIs serve as the essential benchmarks that gauge the success of various initiatives and strategies within the company. Once you determine what those KPIs are, you must then ensure there is a great system to get you the status of the KPIs on an ongoing basis. This system allows leaders to stay informed about current performance levels and identify areas that require immediate attention.

Whether it's revenue and profit numbers, customer satisfaction metrics, or any number of other data points, a leader needs to know how the business is performing in all areas, at all times. This comprehensive understanding enables you to make informed decisions that drive the organization forward. This approach is often called a balanced scorecard because it allows you to balance all the competing priorities against each other to optimize each area. This method ensures that no single area is neglected, promoting overall organizational health and sustainable success. Effective business acumen, therefore, involves not only recognizing what metrics matter most but also continuously monitoring and adjusting strategies to meet these key objectives. At times you'll need to focus more attention on one area than another, but never keeping your eye off all the metrics that matter.

In order to effectively understand each of your KPIs, you must be able to analyze information as it comes in. Understanding how to read the data that matters for your organization is an important skill needed in order to lead an organization. While there is much to be learned about analyzing data, there are four main stages of data analytics that I have found the most helpful; *Descriptive*: information that tells you what has already happened, *Diagnostics*: looking for relationships in the data, *Predictive*: using what you have learned to decide what might happen, and *Prescriptive*: using all that information to decide what course of action you should take. By focusing on the data around each of the KPIs, and adopting a methodical approach to analyzing that data, you are able to dial in on the areas where the team needs to focus.

Leaders need to be able to bring order and control to the complexities of any business. This requires you to have a deep understanding of how the business works, so that you can make key decisions, even in ambiguous situations. When determining what action should be taken, a leader needs to have the data at hand so that the areas that are in greatest need of improvement, get the focus. That makes it easier to communicate a sense of urgency about goals, tasks, and objectives that are pressing and important, rather than urgency around every initiative. This discernment helps in prioritizing efforts and resources effectively, ensuring that the most critical areas receive the attention they need. By doing so, leaders can maintain focus on strategic priorities while preventing burnout and confusion within their teams.

15.   VISION & STRATEGY

Yogi Berra once said, "If you don't know where you are going, you might wind up somewhere else". Once a leader understands what the KPIs are for the business they are running, they then need to set a clear vision for the team to achieve those goals. It is important that everyone on the team understands the mission and goals - people need to know where you are going and why. It is especially important to have a compelling vision that provides direction and focuses everyone's energy on getting where you need them to go. Great leaders are able to help make the connection with their teams, to show how everyone's individual work ties in with the overall goals.

A clear vision should be followed by the creation of a strategy. For example, you might say, "We will achieve XYZ by XYZ date, as measured by XYZ criteria." Here is a simple way to develop a strategy: Start by identifying the overall purpose of your business and write it in the center of a document. Around this central purpose, list the various important activities for your business, such as marketing, customer retention, and employee satisfaction. Next, under each of these activities, note the key ongoing tasks that support your purpose. Also, list the unique aspects of each activity and the value they add. Ensure that each part of the strategy works together, creating a comprehensive plan that outlines what the business can achieve. This approach helps visualize how different activities contribute to the overall goals and ensures alignment in efforts. This method also allows you to visualize how much work is being put towards each area, to ensure the work is balanced.

In many businesses, a portion of the overall strategy is pushed down from a larger segment or division. This hierarchical approach ensures alignment with the broader organizational goals. In those cases, you need to take the division strategy and integrate it with your own unique strategy. This requires a nuanced understanding of both the overarching goals and the specific needs and capabilities of your business. This is an area that is often overlooked when building out an organization's strategy. By showing how the work of your team ties in to broader work from a larger division, you demonstrate a higher-level understanding of the big picture.

The strategy that you set forth for your organization must also be inclusive of ever-changing external factors that could impact the business. Leaders need to keep a finger on the pulse of economic trends, environmental changes, industry developments, and competitive pressures. This vigilance will allow you to anticipate potential challenges and opportunities, and to adjust your strategies accordingly. Get frequent report outs on various external forces that might impact your business. As you learn new information, you can modify any strategies that need to change. Too many leaders fall into the trap of setting their strategies at the beginning of the year, and not keeping an eye on what might be changing in their business environment. Stay one step ahead of your competition, by creating a system to work these changes into your strategy on a continuous basis.

16. SETTING GOALS & EXPECTATIONS

Once a strategy is defined, all attention should go towards executing that strategy. The first step is to align the organization and allocation of resources according to the strategic priorities. All too often, the organization is set up to deliver an *old* set of goals. Just by the nature of the organizational structure, the resources and energy are going towards things that used to matter, or used to be the goals. A simple way to start this process is by laying out your current organization chart, and noting next to each group what goal they are primarily focused on achieving. This will allow you to quickly see where the current focus of your teams is. Then overlay your current strategies and goals, and identify where you are not matched up. Put your resources towards your *current* strategic priorities.

After the organization's resources are stacked up against the strategic priorities, you must translate your strategy into appropriate tactics to achieve the business goals. A simple method that works well is the use of a S.M.A.R.T. action plan. Create a document that lists out each activity, in terms that are *Specific, Measurable, Actionable, Realistic, and Timebound.* Every one of your strategies should have a variety of actions, big and small, that will get you to the achievement of that goal. A goal without a plan is just a dream. The more time and effort you put into creating this document, the more assurance you will have that your strategies aren't just dreams, but rather, that there is a solid plan to achieve each one.

When developing your S.M.A.R.T. plan, always involve your team in the creation of it, to drive buy-in. People tend to defend and support the things that they *personally* helped to create. You simply can't get the same type of buy-in, when the leader has created the plan, and is just pushing it down through the organization. Give each project owner accountability for the items that they are able to impact. Each project owner should then give monthly or quarterly report outs to the broader team on the progress of their actions. Create an environment of agility, so that plans can modify as the work moves, or the business environment changes. These S.M.A.R.T. plans and goals should be focused on achieving results, not checking boxes.

Ensuring that the broader organization knows what actions and projects you are working on, as it relates to your overall strategy, is key. It keeps employees motivated and improves their confidence, as they understand the objectives. Having clear goals helps everyone to focus on priorities. Make sure that each person in your organization knows what the unique expectation of their individual role is. By spelling out the expectations of each person, it creates a culture of accountability. The expectations of each role should tie back to the broader goals of the organization, and they help both the leader and every member of the team to get on the same page. They also serve as a baseline for providing feedback to individuals. By tying current performance levels to the expectations that were previously set, a leader can help each person see where they are excelling or needing improvement.

17.   FUTURISTIC & INNOVATIVE THINKING

Leaders must always be looking to the future to evaluate the competition, the overall market, and the consumer demographic that will be needed in the coming years. In order to do that, you have to keep a pulse on not just the industry that you're in, but also on changing global trends, and understanding what consumers might be looking for in the future. External factors are constantly changing, and a leader needs to be one step ahead, to anticipate how to best position the business as times change. Continually doing things the way you have been, or simply relying on what's worked in the past, is not a formula for success. Instead, your business strategy should always be grounded in today, while pointing towards the things that will make your organization successful in the future.

A tactic that I have used often is to assign each member of my team a specific aspect of 'futuristic thinking', that they are responsible for. I ask them to spend time reading articles on that specific topic, and then report out to the rest of the team occasionally, what they have learned. For example, one person might be in charge of understanding how consumer spending habits are changing from prior years. Another might focus on a completely different industry from ours, to see how a different sector is adapting and changing with the times. I have found some really interesting connections by studying unrelated industries, and decisions they are making about the future.

Along with that focus on futuristic thinking, your team should be thinking often about how to innovate. Innovation can range from significant breakthroughs to smaller upgrades, as long as they help the organization in a new way. Innovation, at the core, is developing and then implementing fresh, new ideas. This often comes in the form of taking an existing product or service and using it in a new way, or adding additional features to make the product or service even better. Innovation is often paired with creativity and courage, as those skills often accompany each other to help create new and different ideas. When your teams feel supported by you to try new ideas out, it can often lead to really interesting new ways of looking at your business.

Encourage your team to bring you their wild ideas to help reinvent your future. It creates an environment where people dream big and think of new solutions to challenges. Innovation and creativity will lead to continuous improvement and energized thinking in your business. When someone brings a new idea, publicly praise them in front of others, so the rest of the team understands the importance of doing the same. Even if the new idea isn't implemented, or it doesn't end up working, your support of the process creates an environment within your organization that focuses on creative thinking to solve problems. When your team is constantly looking at not just today, but also to the future, you set your organization up for longer-term success.

18.   CONTINUOUS IMPROVEMENT

This final step in the leadership journey is the realization that this work never actually ends! Continuous improvement means that you are constantly listening to your customers, constantly looking at data on your KPIs, and constantly improving your standards. It is a never-ending process of working to make the business better. Continuous improvement is not something that you 'do', but rather, it has to be a part of the culture. Empower everyone on the team to always be working to make things better. Your internal processes should always be improving, and your customer-facing processes should as well.

A leader should create the environment where team members are always on the lookout for faster or more cost-effective ways to complete a task. Ensure that there is an easy way for your team to suggest various ideas to improve efficiencies and processes. Embracing a culture of continuous improvement not only drives innovation but also helps maintain a competitive edge in the market. By regularly asking your team what ideas they have to enhance the customer experience, or improve your processes, you create a system of continuous engagement. That in turn helps employees at all levels to feel like they are an integral part of the organization's ongoing success.

Thank you for reading *Lessons in Leadership - Sharing the Wisdom of Great Hotel General Managers.*

Best of luck to you in your leadership journey.

For more leadership tips, please visit: *MarylouiseFitzgibbon.com*